Find Rest

JOURNAL

SHAUNTI FELDHAHN

iDisciple®

Dear Friends,

We live whirlwind lives, don't we? Whether we're juggling work, a family, dating, ministry commitments, friendships, or countless other demands, it's hard to catch a breath. It can be discouraging to have people tell us, "You're so busy—you just need to slow down." Slowing down can be a solution for a short time, but it doesn't feel realistic for a lifetime!

But the amazing truth is that Jesus promises us rest *while we are busy!* He says in Matthew 11:29, "Take my yoke upon you . . . and you will find rest for your souls." A yoke is fastened onto a horse or oxen so they can plow the field in the heat of the day! Jesus doesn't say "Take off the yoke and head back to the barn to find rest." Instead, the promise is that we can find rest for our souls—we can feel that sense of peace, and rightness, and a light burden—in the middle of our normal, busy lives.

This journal is part of the journey of getting to that place of rest, with meaningful scripture and quotes from *Find Rest: A Women's Devotional for Lasting Peace in a Busy Life*, so you can come, think, pray and reflect. This journal stands on its own, but if you haven't already read the devotional, I invite you to connect with God on *those* pages as well.

I'm ready for a life that is busy but feels like rest instead of stress! I know you are too. See you in the garden, friends.

To: ....

From: ....

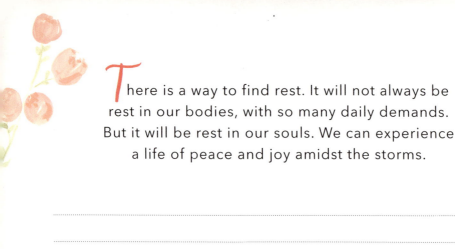

There is a way to find rest. It will not always be rest in our bodies, with so many daily demands. But it will be rest in our souls. We can experience a life of peace and joy amidst the storms.

Truly my soul finds rest in God; my salvation comes from him. Truly he is my rock and my salvation; he is my fortress, I will never be shaken.

PSALM 62:1-2 NIV

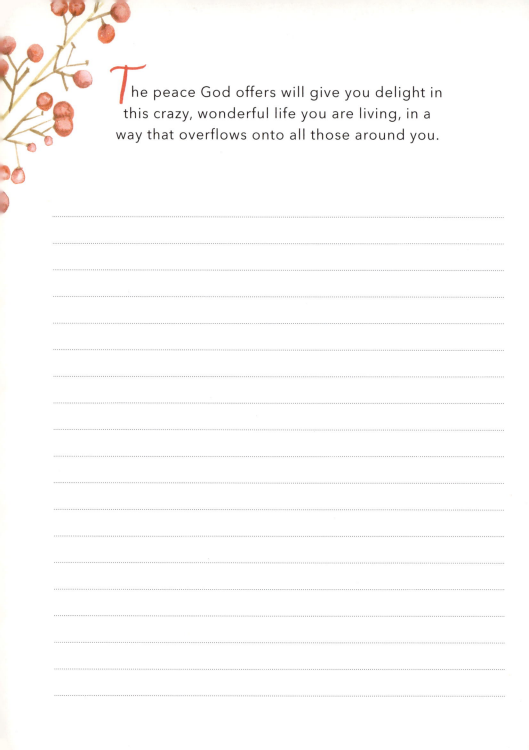

The peace God offers will give you delight in this crazy, wonderful life you are living, in a way that overflows onto all those around you.

*May the God of hope fill you with all joy and
peace as you trust in him, so that you may overflow
with hope by the power of the Holy Spirit.*

ROMANS 15:13 NIV

*L*et's stop looking to temporary signals for a sense of direction. We must look to the One who both never changes and is gentle with our human, frazzled state.

The grass withers and the flowers fade,
but the word of our God stands forever.

ISAIAH 40:8 NLT

So often, we are weary and burdened not because of having too much to do, but because we are taking on things we were never meant to do, or in a way or during a time we were never meant to do them. But when we take up His yoke for us, we will find rest.

....

....

....

....

....

....

....

....

....

....

....

....

....

....

....

....

....

....

....

....

....

Come to me, all you who are weary and burdened, and I will give you rest. Take my yoke upon you and learn from me, for I am gentle and humble in heart, and you will find rest for your souls.

MATTHEW 11:28-29 NIV

*L*et's stop glorifying the busy schedules and giving ourselves a pat on the back when we squeeze one more commitment into an already too-packed day.

We can make our own plans, but the Lord gives the
right answer. People may be pure in their own eyes,
but the Lord examines their motives. Commit your
actions to the Lord, and your plans will succeed.

PROVERBS 16:1-3 NLT

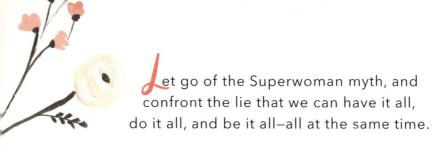

Let go of the Superwoman myth, and confront the lie that we can have it all, do it all, and be it all—all at the same time.

I pray that your love will overflow more and more, and that you will keep on growing in knowledge and understanding. For I want you to understand what really matters, so that you may live pure and blameless lives until the day of Christ's return.

PHILIPPIANS 1:9-10 NLT

*W*e were designed to have to make choices. To prioritize.

Do you have the gift of speaking? Then speak as though God himself were speaking through you. Do you have the gift of helping others? Do it with all the strength and energy that God supplies. Then everything you do will bring glory to God through Jesus Christ.

1 PETER 4:11 NLT

We were not designed
to be Superwomen.

For everything there is a season, a time for every activity under heaven. A time to be born and a time to die. A time to plant and a time to harvest. A time to kill and a time to heal. A time to tear down and a time to build up. A time to cry and a time to laugh. A time to grieve and a time to dance. A time to scatter stones and a time to gather stones. A time to embrace and a time to turn away. A time to search and a time to quit searching. A time to keep and a time to throw away. A time to tear and a time to mend. A time to be quiet and a time to speak. A time to love and a time to hate. A time for war and a time for peace.

ECCLESIASTES 3:1-8 NLT

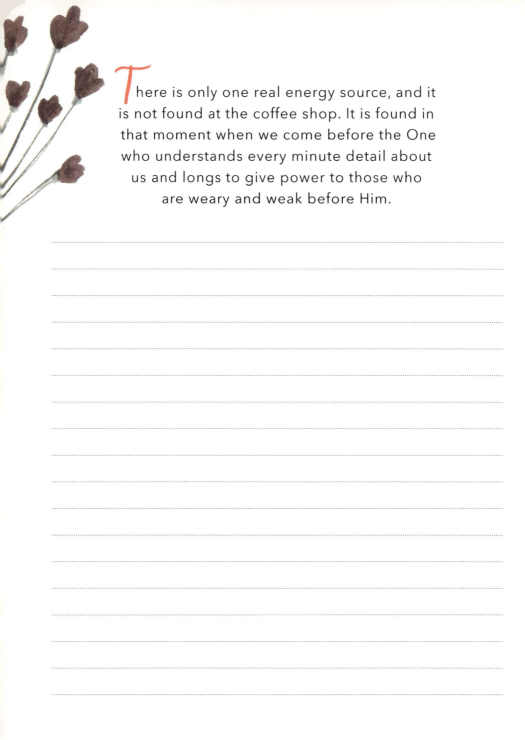

There is only one real energy source, and it is not found at the coffee shop. It is found in that moment when we come before the One who understands every minute detail about us and longs to give power to those who are weary and weak before Him.

Yes, I am the vine; you are the branches. Those who remain in me, and I in them, will produce much fruit. For apart from me you can do nothing.

JOHN 15:5 NLT

*H*e provides guidance and wisdom and
fills every single need of your heart.

He grants a treasure of common sense to the honest. He is a shield to those who walk with integrity. He guards the paths of the just and protects those who are faithful to him.

PROVERBS 2:7-8 NLT

*G*od may not remove the circumstances
that fill up your day, but He will give you
the strength to walk with Him through it.

Teach me to do your will, for you are my God. May your gracious Spirit lead me forward on a firm footing.

PSALM 143:10 NLT

What we focus on will change what we observe around us. We will notice more and more of what we focus on or, conversely, less and less of what we don't want to see.

Do everything without complaining and arguing, so that no one can criticize you. Live clean, innocent lives as children of God, shining like bright lights in a world full of crooked and perverse people.

PHILIPPIANS 2:14-15 NLT

*A*s we focus on "whatever is lovely"—those good and true things we like and appreciate—we'll find ourselves noticing those things more often.

Whatever is true, whatever is noble, whatever is right, whatever is pure, whatever is lovely, whatever is admirable—if anything is excellent or praiseworthy—think about such things.

PHILIPPIANS 4:8 NIV

We were not created to do life alone.

This is my commandment: Love each other in the same way I have loved you. There is no greater love than to lay down one's life for one's friends.

JOHN 15:12-13 NLT

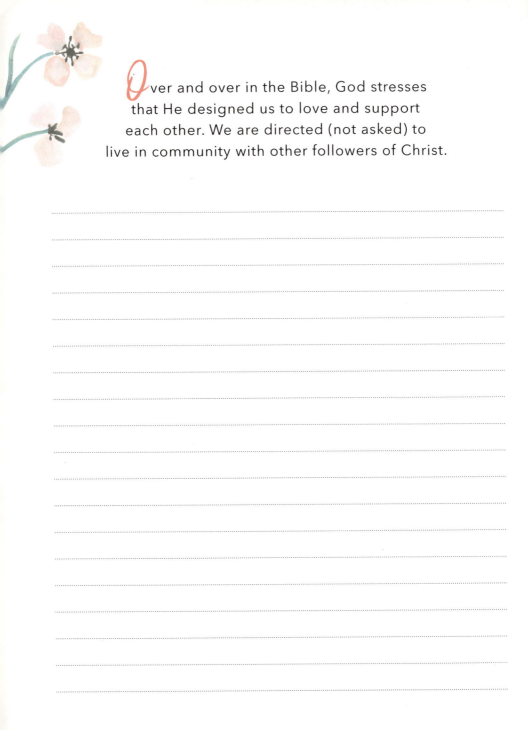

Over and over in the Bible, God stresses that He designed us to love and support each other. We are directed (not asked) to live in community with other followers of Christ.

Love each other with genuine affection, and take delight in honoring each other. Never be lazy, but work hard and serve the Lord enthusiastically. Rejoice in our confident hope. Be patient in trouble, and keep on praying. When God's people are in need, be ready to help them. Always be eager to practice hospitality.

ROMANS 12:10-13 NLT

God has created community for us to call on.
Are you willing to inconvenience a fellow
believer in order to live in authentic community?

....

....

....

....

....

....

....

....

....

....

....

....

....

....

....

....

....

*A friend is always loyal, and a [sister]
is born to help in time of need.*

PROVERBS 17:17 NLT

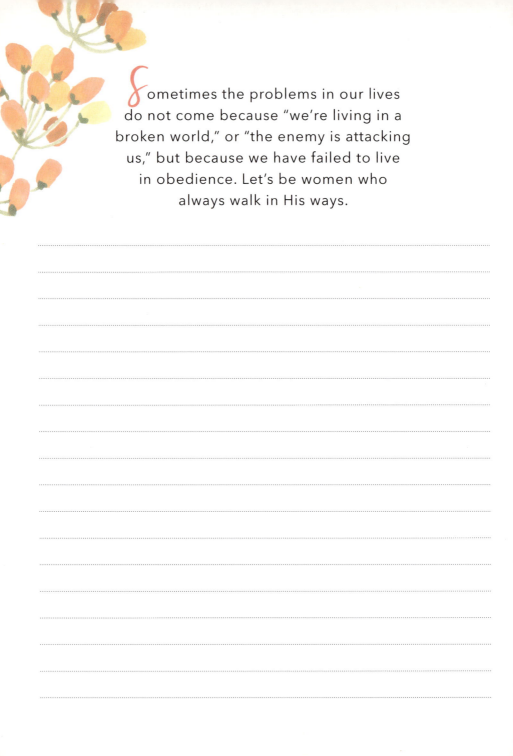

$\mathcal{S}$ometimes the problems in our lives do not come because "we're living in a broken world," or "the enemy is attacking us," but because we have failed to live in obedience. Let's be women who always walk in His ways.

For the grace of God has appeared that offers salvation to all people. It teaches us to say "No" to ungodliness and worldly passions, and to live self-controlled, upright and godly lives in this present age, while we wait for the blessed hope—the appearing of the glory of our great God and Savior, Jesus Christ.

TITUS 2:11-13 NIV

*O*ur stories are woven with many threads, including joy, worry, struggle, happiness, and—since we can't know what will happen tomorrow—the great unknown. But as Christ followers, we do know the ending of our story.

Don't be afraid, for I am with you. Don't be discouraged,
for I am your God. I will strengthen you and help you.
I will hold you up with my victorious right hand.

ISAIAH 41:10 NLT

In the end, God will defeat everything that makes us sad, scared, or defeated. We can't see eternity yet, but we can cling to the truth that once and for all, God does win against the enemy. And as children of God, we win too.

He will wipe every tear from their eyes. There will be no more death or mourning or crying or pain, for the old order of things has passed away ... I am making everything new!

REVELATION 21:4-5 NIV

*N*o matter the activity—big or small, fascinating or boring—God uses us where we are. We can be a testament to his goodness everywhere.

We now have this light shining in our hearts, but we ourselves are like fragile clay jars containing this great treasure. This makes it clear that our great power is from God, not from ourselves.

2 CORINTHIANS 4:7 NLT

*I*nstead of looking through the lens that shows the most unflattering perspective, let's choose the one that changes everything. That lens is called gratitude. Gratitude for everything God has allowed us to have that is good, and gratitude that He is sufficient.

....

....

....

....

....

....

....

....

....

....

....

....

....

....

....

....

....

....

....

....

Let your roots grow down into him, and let your lives be built on him. Then your faith will grow strong in the truth you were taught, and you will overflow with thankfulness.

COLOSSIANS 2:7 NLT

*H*e wants you to come to Him just as you are, before you have anything figured out. He loves you when you are broken, empty, with nothing to give. Poor in spirit.

He heals the brokenhearted and bandages their wounds. He counts the stars and calls them all by name. How great is our Lord! His power is absolute! His understanding is beyond comprehension!

PSALM 147:3-5 NLT

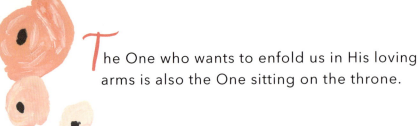

The One who wants to enfold us in His loving arms is also the One sitting on the throne.

This is the confidence we have in approaching God;
that if we ask anything according to his will, he hears us.

1 JOHN 5:14 NIV

We are called to rescue the captives bound for destruction, to be agents of light in a kingdom of darkness.

"You are the light of the world—like a city on a hilltop that cannot be hidden . . . In the same way, let your good deeds shine out for all to see, so that everyone will praise your heavenly Father.

MATTHEW 5:14;16 NLT

*R*esolve to notice each day, and be glad in it.

....
....
....
....
....
....
....
....
....
....
....
....
....
....
....
....

This is the day the Lord has made.
We will rejoice and be glad in it.

PSALM 118:24 NLT

*C*elebrating who we are—and
are not—is the key to fitting joyfully
into our place in the body of Christ.

God has placed the parts in the body, every one of them, just as he wanted them to be. . . . Now you are the body of Christ, and each one of you is a part of it.

1 CORINTHIANS 12:18; 27 NIV

It feels risky, even embarrassing, to ask for help. But the beauty of allowing someone to help us as we limp toward the finish line is that it reminds us that we are never, ever alone.

Don't just pretend to love others. Really love them. Hate what is wrong. Hold tightly to what is good. Love each other with genuine affection, and take delight in honoring each other.

ROMANS 12:9-10 NLT

*W*e must not feel bad for devoting ourselves
to the season God has called us into.

And whatever you do, whether in word or deed,
do it all in the name of the Lord Jesus, giving
thanks to God the Father through him.

COLOSSIANS 3:17 NIV

*L*et's commit to praying for wisdom to know what God is calling us to do right now to bring Him glory in our particular season.

The Lord will guide you continually, giving you water when you are dry and restoring your strength. You will be like a well-watered garden, like an ever-flowing spring.

ISAIAH 58:11 NLT

Scripture says that if we resist the devil, he will flee. The only way to do that is to draw close to God.

Be to me a rock of refuge, to which I may continually
come; you have given the command to save me,
for you are my rock and my fortress.

PSALM 71:3 ESV

*W*hen we come near to God,
He promises to come near to us.

*But if from there you seek the Lord your God, you will find him
if you look for him with all your heart and with all your soul.*

DEUTERONOMY 4:29 NIV

I think we often forget that we are beloved daughters of God. He adores us and longs for us to come to Him and boldly ask Him for help.

I sought the Lord, and he answered me and delivered me from all my fears. Those who look to him are radiant and their faces shall never be ashamed.

PSALM 34:4-5 ESV

*W*e so often feel battered and bruised. Our hearts feel hurt by relationships that disappoint us. Our minds struggle to keep anxiety at bay. Our bodies feel tired and pulled in a hundred different directions. Let's have the confidence and vulnerability to trust that if we run boldly to God's throne, He will respond with open arms.

And I am convinced that nothing can ever separate us from God's love. Neither death nor life, neither angels nor demons, neither our fears for today nor our worries about tomorrow—not even the powers of hell can separate us from God's love. No power in the sky above or in the earth below—indeed, nothing in all creation will ever be able to separate us from the love of God that is revealed in Christ Jesus our Lord.

ROMANS 8:38-39 NLT

*D*are to trust your Father with your heart.
You will find grace in your time of need.

....
....
....
....
....
....
....
....
....
....
....
....
....
....
....

For I am about to do something new. See, I have already begun! Do you not see it? I will make a pathway through the wilderness. I will create rivers in the dry wasteland.

ISAIAH 43:19 NLT

*I*f Jesus was willing to pass up the multitude and trust in His Father's plan, we need to be able to pass up multitudes of opportunities—good things!—in the same way. Then we can do the one thing God is doing.

Unless the Lord builds the house, the builders labor in vain. Unless the Lord watches over the city, the guards stand watch in vain.

PSALM 127:1 NIV

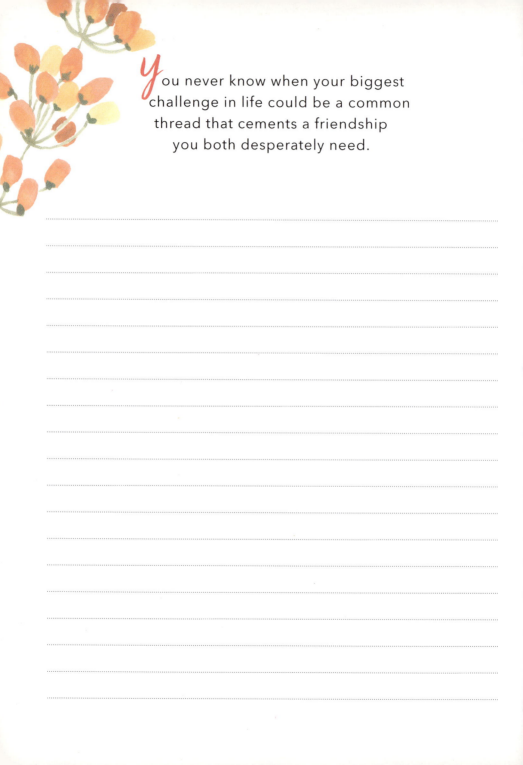

You never know when your biggest
challenge in life could be a common
thread that cements a friendship
you both desperately need.

Two are better than one, because they have a good return for their labor: If either of them falls down, one can help the other up. But pity anyone who falls and has no one to help them up.

ECCLESIASTES 4:9-10 NIV

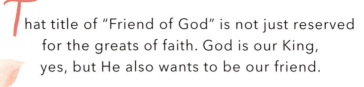

That title of "Friend of God" is not just reserved for the greats of faith. God is our King, yes, but He also wants to be our friend.

_____
_____
_____
_____
_____
_____
_____
_____
_____
_____
_____
_____
_____
_____
_____
_____
_____
_____

*I have called you friends, for everything that I learned
from my Father I have made known to you. You did not
choose me, but I chose you and appointed you so that
you might go and bear fruit—fruit that will last—and so
that whatever you ask in my name the Father will give you.*

JOHN 15:15-16 NIV

Choose to trust God as your best friend, the One who will always do what is best for you. He is the friend who will never let you down.

Let me hear of your unfailing love each morning, for I am trusting you. Show me where to walk, for I give myself to you.

PSALM 143:8 NLT

We do have idols today, and it is one of the main reasons for the stress and worry in our lives. Idols are anything other than God that we rely or lean on for support—but they will never support us well.

Of what value is an idol carved by a craftsman? Or an image that teaches lies? For the one who makes it trusts in [her] own creation; [she] makes idols that cannot speak. Woe to [her] who says to wood, "come to life!" Or to lifeless stone, "Wake up!" Can it give guidance? It is covered with gold and silver; there is no breath in it.

HABAKKUK 2:18-19 NIV

*L*et's depend on God with our entire heart, soul, strength and mind. He's the only one who can hold us up.

The Lord is trustworthy in all his promises and faithful in all he does. The Lord upholds all who fall down and lifts up all who are bowed down.

PSALM 145:13-14 NIV

*I*n the right time, we thrive.

*For God is working in you, giving you the
desire and the power to do what pleases him.*

PHILIPPIANS 2:13 NLT

What we focus on can either steal our joy or build it.

If you search for good, you will find favor;
but if you search for evil, it will find you!

PROVERBS 11:27 NLT

If we're going to emulate anyone's life, let it be His.

Imitate God, therefore, in everything you do, because you are his dear children. Live a life filled with love, following the example of Christ. He loved us and offered himself as a sacrifice for us, a pleasing aroma to God.

EPHESIANS 5:1-2 NLT

*S*ometimes we need to realize that there are some fights God does not want us to take on. They are His.

The Lord will fight for you; you need only to be still.

EXODUS 14:14 NIV

We have to not only retrain our brains to focus on what is good and lovely about others, but to say what is good and lovely about others.

Since God chose you to be the holy people he loves, you must clothe yourselves with tenderhearted mercy, kindness, humility, gentleness, and patience. Make allowance for each other's faults, and forgive anyone who offends you. Remember, the Lord forgave you, so you must forgive others. Above all, clothe yourselves with love, which binds us all together in perfect harmony.

COLOSSIANS 3:12-14 NLT

*M*any of us are literally running on adrenaline instead of a healthy foundation of rest, deep breaths, prayer time, God-directed pacing, and peace.

*Don't you realize that your body is the temple of the
Holy Spirit, who lives in you and was given to you by God?
You do not belong to yourself, for God bought you with a
high price. So you must honor God with your body.*

1 CORINTHIANS 6:19-20 NLT

*J*ust as you need oxygen to fuel your body, you need deep soul breaths of God's Word. He will restore your soul.

The instructions of the Lord are perfect, reviving the soul . . . the decrees of the Lord are trustworthy, making wise the simple. The commandments of the Lord are right, bringing joy to the heart. The commands of the Lord are clear, giving insight for living. . . . They are more desirable than gold, even the finest gold. They are sweeter than honey, even honey dripping from the comb.

PSALM 19:7-8; 10 NLT

Often a judgmental or a fearful spirit requires energy and creates emotional baggage we were not meant to carry.

And let the peace that comes from Christ rule in your hearts. For as members of one body you are called to live in peace. And always be thankful.

COLOSSIANS 3:15 NLT

The busyness of our lives can often feel hopeless because the enemy of our souls wants us to think it is hopeless. But it's not!

Cry out for insight, and ask for understanding. Search for them as you would for silver; seek them like hidden treasures. Then you will understand what it means to fear the LORD, and you will gain knowledge of God.

PROVERBS 2:3-5 NLT

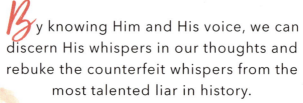

By knowing Him and His voice, we can discern His whispers in our thoughts and rebuke the counterfeit whispers from the most talented liar in history.

Don't be deceived, my dear brothers and sisters. Every good and perfect gift is from above, coming down from the Father of the heavenly lights, who does not change like shifting shadows.

JAMES 1:16-17 NIV

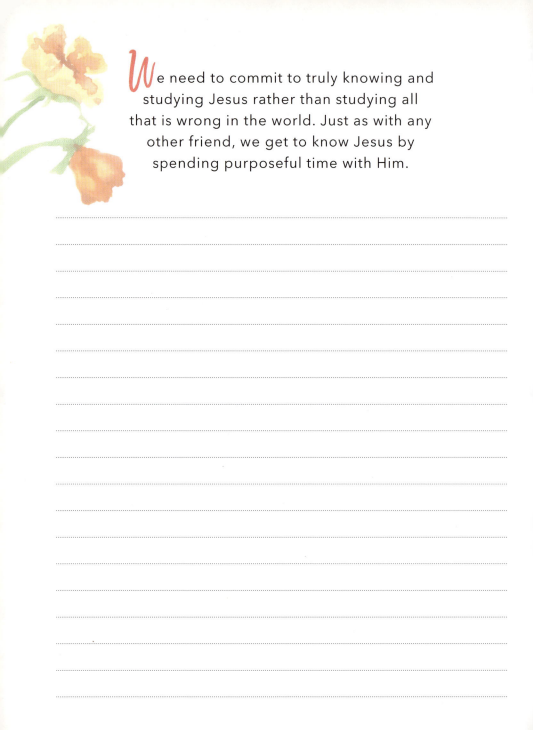

We need to commit to truly knowing and studying Jesus rather than studying all that is wrong in the world. Just as with any other friend, we get to know Jesus by spending purposeful time with Him.

*Yes, everything else is worthless when compared with
the infinite value of knowing Christ Jesus my Lord.*

PHILIPPIANS 3:8 NLT

*K*nowing Jesus as the real deal will help us focus more on what He is doing and less on the distractions of the enemy.

*But those who wish to boast should boast in this
alone: that they truly know me and understand that I
am the Lord who demonstrates unfailing love and
who brings justice and righteousness to the earth,
and that I delight in these things.*

JEREMIAH 9:24 NLT

We can't always trust our feelings. But we can trust the compass of God's Word. You may be feeling abandoned or worried, but the Bible clearly says God is always with us so we do not need to be afraid. We need to trust that those words are 100 percent true—and act like it.

The Lord himself goes before you and will be with you; he will never leave you nor forsake you. Do not be afraid; do not be discouraged.

DEUTERONOMY 31:8 NIV

God loves you for you, because you are His, and it doesn't matter if tomorrow you accomplish one thing or twenty. Nothing will cause Him to love you less or more.

For the Lord your God is living among you. He is a mighty savior.
He will take delight in you with gladness. With his love, he will
calm all your fears. He will rejoice over you with joyful songs.

ZEPHANIAH 3:17 NLT

*I*sn't it just like Jesus to
take our deepest regrets
and wipe them clean?

Have mercy on me, O God, because of your unfailing love.
Because of your great compassion, blot out the stain of my sins.
Wash me clean from my guilt. Purify me from my sin.

PSALM 51:1-2 NLT

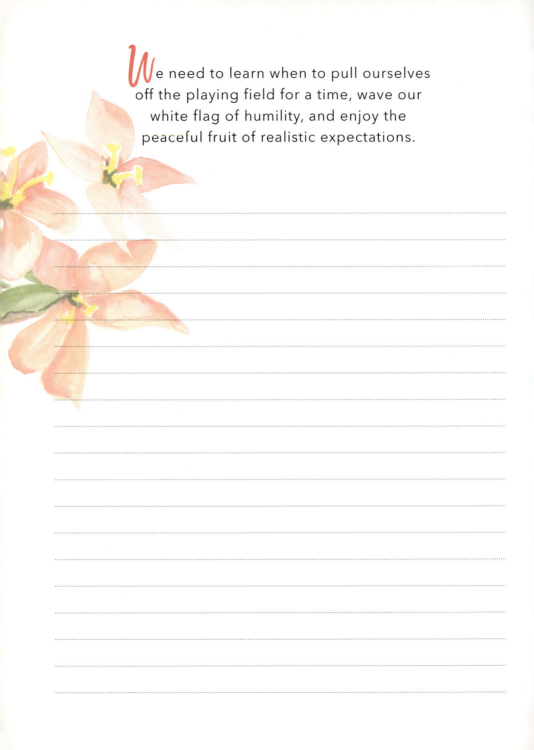

We need to learn when to pull ourselves off the playing field for a time, wave our white flag of humility, and enjoy the peaceful fruit of realistic expectations.

Trust in the Lord with all your heart, and do not lean on your own understanding. In all your ways acknowledge him, and he will make straight your paths.

PROVERBS 3:5-6 ESV

*G*od never gives us a calling without providing all we need to get it done, and that includes time and emotional capacity. If we aren't able to get it done, despite our best efforts, then He has a different plan in mind.

Yet God has made everything beautiful for its own time. He has planted eternity in the human heart, but even so, people cannot see the whole scope of God's work from beginning to end.

ECCLESIASTES 3:11 NLT

*L*et's listen when the Holy Spirit gently calls us to set certain things aside and trust that He has them in His control.

Those who listen to instruction will prosper;
those who trust the Lord will be joyful.

PROVERBS 16:20 NLT

*O*ur God loves us. He will not always take us out of our circumstances, but He will always meet our needs in those circumstances. To believe and trust in Him, to be intentionally grateful even in legitimately difficult times, is one of the highest forms of praise and thanksgiving. It produces joy.

Always be joyful. Never stop praying. Be thankful in all circumstances, for this is God's will for you who belong to Christ Jesus.

1 THESSALONIANS 5:16-18 NLT

The key to living a cheerful
life is choosing gratitude.

And whatever you do or say, do it as a representative of the Lord Jesus, giving thanks through him to God the Father.

COLOSSIANS 3:17 NLT

Transforming gratitude chooses to view the glass as half full, to intentionally repeat the positive rather than the negative, to focus on the one piece of good news amidst a cluster of bad. Transforming gratitude chooses to believe the best about someone, to overlook minor offenses rather than magnify them. Transforming gratitude is not always easy, but it is a choice any of us can make.

That is why we never give up. Though our bodies are dying, our spirits are being renewed every day. For our present troubles are small and won't last very long. Yet they produce for us a glory that vastly outweighs them and will last forever!

2 CORINTHIANS 4:16-17 NLT

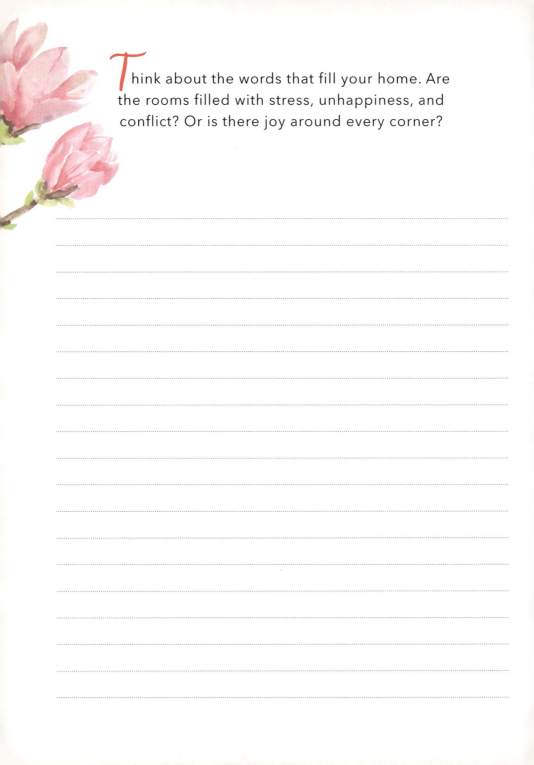

Think about the words that fill your home. Are the rooms filled with stress, unhappiness, and conflict? Or is there joy around every corner?

*Kind words are like honey– sweet to
the soul and healthy for the body.*

PROVERBS 16:24 NLT

God is always there, and always moving, it's just that we don't always notice. Our lives will change forever once we resolve to not miss God's hand in our ascent from the darkness.

Jesus said to them, "My Father is always at work to this very day, and I too am working."

JOHN 5:17 NIV

Jesus is not shocked by our human doubt. He understands. We can be vulnerable enough to cry out our belief in Him while at the same time begging for increased faith.

"Anything is possible if a person believes." The father instantly cried out, "I do believe, but help me overcome my unbelief!"

MARK 9:23-24 NLT

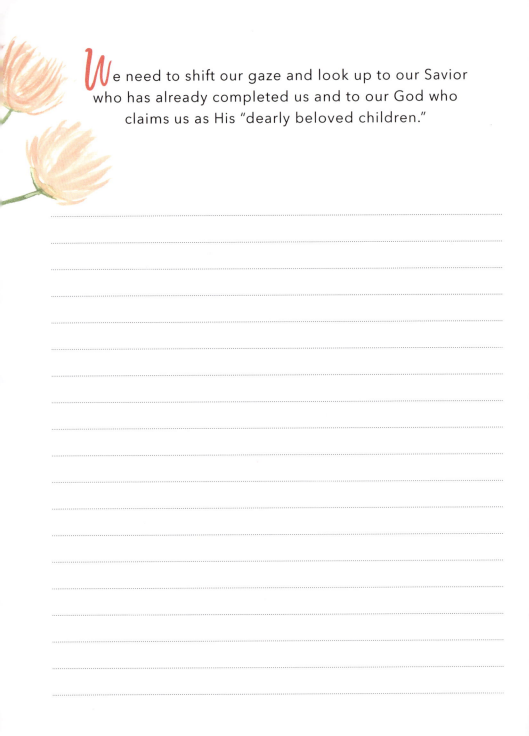

We need to shift our gaze and look up to our Savior who has already completed us and to our God who claims us as His "dearly beloved children."

I prayed to the Lord, and he answered me. He freed me from all my fears. Those who look to him for help will be radiant with joy; no shadow of shame will darken their faces.

PSALM 34:4-5 NLT

We are complete in Christ. When we feel bad—not beautiful, not loved, not enough—and are tempted to look around for fulfillment, let's instead choose to stop and look up to our Savior. Let's ask Him to fill those longings in our hearts, and rest as He does just that.

*You have searched me, Lord, and you know me. You
know when I sit and when I rise; you perceive my
thoughts from afar. You discern my going out and
my lying down; you are familiar with all my ways.
Before a word is on my tongue you, Lord, know it
completely. You hem me in behind and before,
and you lay your hand upon me. Such knowledge
is too wonderful for me, too lofty for me to attain.*

PSALM 139:1-6 NIV

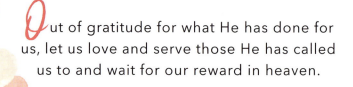

*O*ut of gratitude for what He has done for us, let us love and serve those He has called us to and wait for our reward in heaven.

Work hard to show the results of your salvation, obeying God with deep reverence and fear. For God is working in you, giving you the desire and the power to do what pleases him.

PHILIPPIANS 2:12-13 NLT

We desperately need to be in touch with God, both out of love for Him and His love for us.

Let the word of Christ dwell in you richly.

COLOSSIANS 3:16 ESV

*W*e must be careful not to become prideful and dissatisfied when we play the comparison game. Because that is the enemy's game, not God's.

Some people, eager for money, have wandered from the faith and pierced themselves with many griefs. But you, [woman] of God, flee from all this, and pursue righteousness, godliness, faith, love, endurance and gentleness. Fight the good fight of faith. Take hold of the eternal life to which you were called.

1 TIMOTHY 6:10-12 NIV

God od made us unique, and He has a perfect plan for each of us because of our uniqueness.

You are a chosen people. You are royal priests, a holy nation, God's very own possession. As a result, you can show others the goodness of God, for he called you out of the darkness into his wonderful light.

1 PETER 2:9 NLT

*L*et's accept how we each are made,
fearfully and wonderfully, and embrace
the plan that God has designed just for us.

For you created my inmost being; you knit me together in my mother's womb. I praise you because I am fearfully and wonderfully made.

PSALM 139:13-14 NIV

When we are keeping anything hidden in the darkness, especially unconfessed sin, we cannot live the authentic, abundant, joyful life God wants us to have. God is faithful to forgive and restore us if we set aside our pride and come into the light.

*Create in me a clean heart, O God,
and renew a right spirit within me.*

PSALM 51:10 ESV

*W*hat if we could let go of our inhibitions, take more risks, and trust God? We might discover—He is there.

Do not fear, for I have redeemed you; I have summoned you by name; you are mine. When you pass through the waters, I will be with you; and when you pass through the rivers, they will not sweep over you. When you walk through the fire, you will not be burned; the flames will not set you ablaze. For I am the Lord your God.

ISAIAH 43:1-3 NIV

*C*ircumstances in our lives will
change, but God never will.

Jesus Christ is the same yesterday and today and forever.

HEBREWS 13:8 NLT

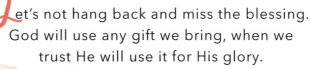

Let's not hang back and miss the blessing.
God will use any gift we bring, when we
trust He will use it for His glory.

....

....

....

....

....

....

....

....

....

....

....

....

....

....

....

....

Now you should finish what you started. Let the eagerness you showed in the beginning be matched now by your giving. Give in proportion to what you have. Whatever you give is acceptable if you give it eagerly. And give according to what you have, not what you don't have.

2 CORINTHIANS 8:11-12 NLT

The Scriptures are full of examples of God embracing the exhausted, weak, sorrowful wanderer. He longs to show you compassion.

....
....
....
....
....
....
....
....
....
....
....
....
....
....
....
....
....
....

The Spirit helps us in our weakness. We do not know what we ought to pray for, but the Spirit himself intercedes for us through wordless groans. And he who searches our hearts knows the mind of the Spirit, because the Spirit intercedes for God's people in accordance with the will of God.

ROMANS 8:26-27 NIV

*C*ome as you are, be transparent,
and express your feelings to Him just
as you would confide in a friend.

I have called you friends, for everything that I learned from my Father I have made know to you.

JOHN 15:15 NIV

God asks us to make a choice: to respond in the opposite way our hearts want to go. Think the best of others, not the worst. Let offenses go. Bless others.

A generous person will prosper; whoever refreshes others will be refreshed.

PROVERBS 11:25 NIV

*A*mazingly, our God has made every one of us important to His purposes. He has made each of us members of the body of Christ. And He uses us to accomplish His work.

So it is with Christ's body. We are many parts of one body, and we all belong to each other. In his grace, God has given us different gifts for doing certain things well.

ROMANS 12:5-6 NLT

*G*od knows every part of us, and He loves us exactly where we are. Part of the privilege of loving others is displaying the same type of love.

*I am writing to remind you, dear friends,
that we should love one another. This
is not a new commandment but one
we have had from the beginning.*

2 JOHN 1:5 NLT

We need to be willing to let Jesus tug on our heart and show us the hearts of those around us. That is one of the key ways to redirect our focus from our to-do list to our most crucial callings.

You, my brothers and sisters, were called to be free. But do not use your freedom to indulge the flesh; rather, serve one another humbly in love. For the entire law is fulfilled in keeping this one command: "Love your neighbor as yourself."

GALATIANS 5:13-14 NIV

By ignoring where God is calling us, we often dive deeper and deeper into stress and weariness, because at that moment we are taking up the wrong yoke and laboring under it.

Don't copy the behavior and customs of this world, but let God transform you into a new person by changing the way you think. Then you will learn to know God's will for you, which is good and pleasing and perfect.

ROMANS 12:2 NLT

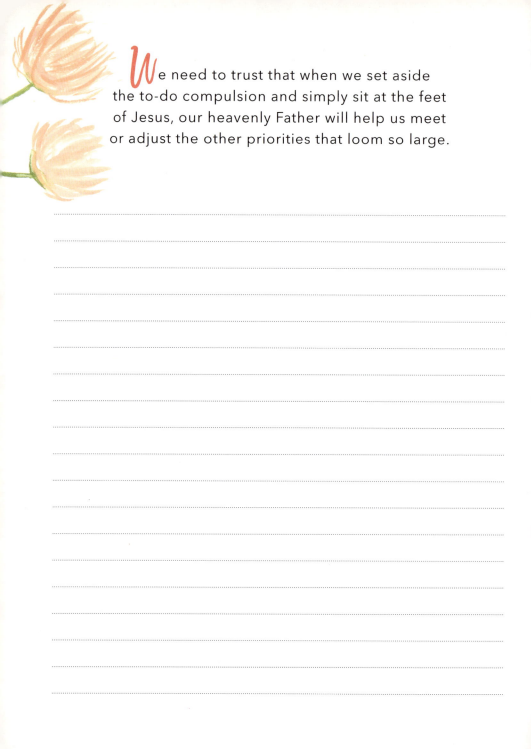

We need to trust that when we set aside the to-do compulsion and simply sit at the feet of Jesus, our heavenly Father will help us meet or adjust the other priorities that loom so large.

So there is a special rest still waiting for the people of God. For all who have entered into God's rest have rested from their labors, just as God did after creating the world. So let us do our best to enter that rest.

HEBREWS 4:9-11 NLT

You can't change the force or trajectory of the storm, but you can change everything about how you experience it.

Consider it pure joy, my brothers and sisters, whenever you face trials of many kinds, because you know that the testing of your faith produces perseverance. Let perseverance finish its work so that you may be mature and complete, not lacking anything.

JAMES 1:2-4 NIV

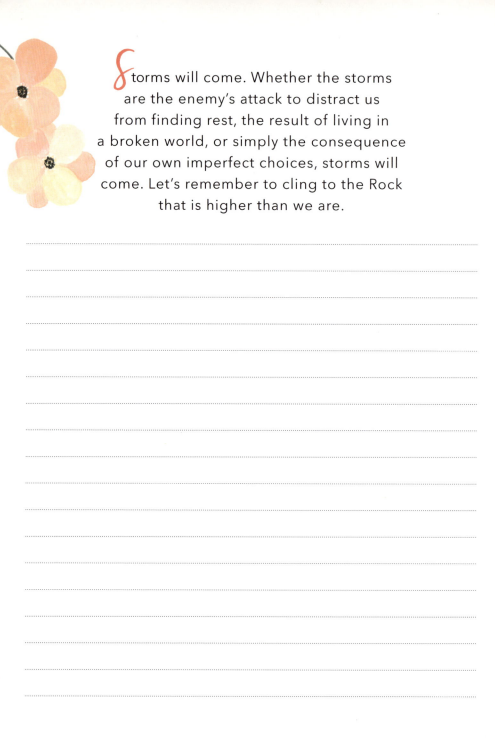

Storms will come. Whether the storms are the enemy's attack to distract us from finding rest, the result of living in a broken world, or simply the consequence of our own imperfect choices, storms will come. Let's remember to cling to the Rock that is higher than we are.

*He calmed the storm to a whisper and stilled
the waves. What a blessing was that stillness
as he brought them safely into harbor!*

PSALM 107:29-30 NLT

*W*e don't have four or five or ten roles—we have one: To be a minister of God's love and grace to everyone we meet.

We are therefore Christ's ambassadors, as though God were making his appeal through us. We implore you on Christ's behalf: Be reconciled to God. God made him who had no sin to be sin for us, so that in him we might become the righteousness of God.

2 CORINTHIANS 5:20-21 NIV